LIT CANNON

LIT CANNON

A Sampler From Mad Zebra Press

ADAM DOVE
KATIE TARBELL
CHRIS ELLIOTT
SYBIL WILEN
HEATHER RICHMOND
KIM SEDLOCK

Mad Zebra Press

Copyright © 2021 by Mad Zebra Press
143 Saint Louis Avenue
Buffalo, New York 14211

!((!

The story "I Was Born in Nineteen Seventy ... Whatever" by Sybil Wilen previously appeared in Burnt Pine Magazine, Issue Five, Winter 2019

All rights reserved. No part of this book may be reproduced in any manner whatsoever without written permission except in the case of brief quotations embodied in critical articles and reviews.

First Printing, 2021

ISBN: 978-0-578-78325-3

Contents

I

Expect Us to Meet in the Dark by Adam Dove

When I was young, my father loved telling me stories about Edison. Old Alva, he called him. He considered himself an amateur historian, my father, and Old Alva was a favorite subject of his.

"Know what he said?" he asked, his back to where I sat among the crickets behind the chapel he'd built himself, rubbing the hem of my Easter dress through the dirt and imagining my mother's face when she learned her husband had let me sit in mud. "When he finally got it lit, after all those years of trying, know what he said?"

His head and shoulders were lost through a cut-out in the back wall of the chapel he'd built, hooking this cable to that node. Testing circuits. I was just seven years old, and he may as well have been rewiring God. All around, the fields glowed dim with the eerie incandescence of twilight. I waved my hands through the air, swatting at fireflies.

"Too bright," he said. He pulled himself from the chipped white wall and stretched to his full height. The sinews of his arms stood out like wires beneath his flesh. "The man's staring the future full in the face, and he thinks the damn thing is too bright!"

He had one of those smiles: touched others' like a lit torch. We sat grinning at the fields until he bubbled over—his deep, booming laughter rolled like thunder over the surrounding fields; his crooked, golden smile lit the countryside like the noon-day sun.

The night she took me away, we ate dinner from a can. Not because my mother was a particularly bad cook, but everything in the house had been Dad's, and when we left, the food had stayed. On the floor of the empty living room, I huddled close to the uncovered bulb of a table lamp set in the carpet, warming my hands in its glow. The air tinged unfamiliar, the fading warmth of another family. I spooned cold spaghetti from the half-opened can in my lap while my mother paced the length of the room, her hair throwing tentacled shadows on the ceiling. Pounding heel prints on the carpet, she counted down the list of his dirty laundry: that drunk, damn irresponsible, that disgusting, half-cocked smile. But I refused to listen, shaking my head no, saying no, under my breath, then louder, no, no—but she walked over my words. I cemented my jaws with canned spaghetti. The scrape of plastic fork on ridged aluminum. She knelt in front of me.

"You're a smart girl Audrey." She grabbed my face in her hands. "Brighter than I ever was. Promise you won't let anyone take it away from you."

"I'm not bright," I said. "I want to go home."

But she was already up, mumbling to herself, painting the ceiling in shadows.

You're a smart girl, Audrey. Never forget. You're a smart girl.

I was twelve when my mother decided I was old enough to spend a weekend unsupervised—a privilege that, up to that point, I had only read about in books. It was as if she was afraid to take her eyes off of me for too long, for fear he might come for me, take me back to the country, back home.

As soon as her car disappeared over the hill, I was out the door and off to the bus station. I'd been stashing away birthday money and bits of allowance for years, and had just enough for the round trip ticket, a Snickers from the vending machine, cab fare, and the five dollars I gave the Amish family who offered to take me the rest of the way, bouncing on the hard wooden seat of their buggy.

I arrived just before dusk, the sun's daily descent just picking up steam. The chapel still stood alone, a bit dustier than I remembered, but there. Thin clouds of insects colored the air, later revealing themselves as fireflies, their dormant bulbs dim in the face of the day's dying embers. A figure in overalls sat low on the front steps, his arms draped over the crux of his knees, the brim of a baseball cap shading his eyes. There was a cardboard box at his feet. As I approached, he plunged his hand into the box and stirred, drawing from its mouth a sound like tinkling icicles.

"I need to speak to the pastor."

He stopped his rummaging and looked up. Beneath the shade of the brim, his eyes were brown and soft as rabbit fur. His face tanned and prickled like cactus flesh.

"Well then, you'll have a while to wait."

"Can you just get him? I'm his daughter."

There was something about the way that sounded I didn't expect: a swollen-tongued, hard-to-get-out feeling.

"How can our pastor have a daughter when we don't even have a pastor?"

He smiled, but not to me, and returned to stirring his box, the sound seeming more abrasive than before, like the gnashing of teeth. Curious, I leaned over and looked inside. Light bulbs, maybe fifty of them, some of them broken, some whole, round and flat and u-shaped all thrown in together. Behind the box, there was a pile of four or five of them between his legs that rolled around like a colony of glass eyes, looking for something.

"Pastor Hunt." I said. "Jeremiah Hunt – this is his church. He built it with his own hands."

My mouth had gone dry and I crossed my arms, hoping he wouldn't see my heart beating out against my shirt.

"Jeremiah Hunt ain't been pastor here for a while now. Moved on a couple years back. Said the Lord was calling him elsewhere."

He removed his arm from the box and all went momentarily quiet. He had a lightbulb clutched in his hand, which he raised up and shook beside his ear. He must have heard something I couldn't, something he didn't like, because he frowned and tossed the bulb back into the box where it shattered on impact. The sound of his searching resumed.

"What exactly are you doing?" I said.

"The show's got to go on," he said, "even without a pastor. You don't expect us to meet in the dark, do you?"

He chuckled, but the rattle of his tobacco-stained laughter cut short as he snapped his hand to his mouth. Face twisted in pain, he sucked the tip of his middle finger between his dusty lips. When he removed it, blood seeped slow through the cracks of his fingerprint. He painted it on the side on the box before plunging in with his other hand, rough as before.

"What will you do when these run out?" I asked. "Why don't you just buy more?"

"Missy," he said, laughing. "You obviously don't know much about the church. No, suppose we'll go on using these until they're all used up. Then we'll meet by candlelight. Got enough of those to last until judgment day."

Alongside the din of tinkling glass, a chorus of crickets had begun to scratch their mating calls out across the empty fields. The sun had only just started to lose itself behind the hills at the back of the lot, and the twinkling of the fireflies was slowly becoming visible. They blinked in and out, Christmas lights suspended on the wind. These were the nights I'd dreamed about. This was the sky I had missed. What she told me we were better off without: the heavens so wide, day and night fit together like puzzle pieces. From my city bedroom window, it seemed barely big enough for the power lines.

I tried to picture the look on my mother's face if she came home and discovered I was gone. What she would do if I never came back. He must have known I'd come looking for him. Why would he just leave?

"When he shows up, will you let him know I came asking for him?"

He removed his hand from the box and sighed.

"Sweetheart, he ain't coming back."

All those years, my mother was so worried, kept such a close eye. Never let me out of her sight. She could have gone to Vegas a hundred times over. She could have moved to Alaska. I would have still been there, gazing out my bedroom window, staring at power lines. Waiting for a sunrise that was never going to come.

The day before my junior prom, I came home from school to find a letter open on the kitchen table saying that my uncle Terry was dead. She would do this sometimes, my mother, whenever bad news came up. Like she wanted me to feel I was breaking it to her, as if it would force me to be strong. When I was ten she left the body of my cat on the living room couch for me to find – his stomach flat and deflated, bulging eyes like dim bulbs of glass. It was only after I got him into the bag and put out by the curb that she said anything.

"I know, honey. He was such a soft cat." Then, "I'm thinking stir fry for dinner?"

Or the day she changed my name back to hers: just left the finished forms on the table, planting her flag firmly in the soil of my life.

I hadn't seen my uncle in over a decade, but holding the envelope then, the sight of him laughing came suddenly to my mind – always hidden behind his mitten hand. The envelope was simple; the letter a sheet of printer paper. *I am sad to say that our dear Terry Hunt has gone to meet the Lord.*

"Mom?" I peeked my head around the corner into the living room, but she was nowhere in sight. "Uncle Terry's dead." I walked through the house, letter in hand. "Mom?"

It was mid-afternoon, but the blackout curtains drawn on every window kept the sunlight at bay. Replaced instead by the unrelenting hum of years collecting lamps in every imaginable incarnation: floor and table, crook and gooseneck. They peppered every inch of the house like bullet holes, coated every flat surface like a mold.

Before too long I found her upstairs, hunched in her chair, reading in the artificial glow.

"Mom. Uncle Terry's dead. Did you see?"

She didn't look up from her book.

"I did, honey. It's sad. He was so good in the kitchen."

I searched the letter again, expecting to see something else on the sheet, maybe a watermark or a code in invisible ink, but there was nothing. Only the words saying he was dead, a few brief prayers, and where to find the funeral. I hadn't seen my grandmother's handwriting since middle school, when the letters stopped. I wanted to sniff it, to see if it smelled like I remembered her, empty ashtrays and pie crust.

"Mom. Do you think...?"

I hadn't considered it before then, but it only made sense that he would be there. After all, Terry was his brother.

"Honestly, honey, I doubt that man would go to his own funeral."

I remember saying something – maybe a soft *right* – but it must not have been enough for her, because she put her hand on my knee where I stood, her eyes still in her book.

"I don't want you thinking about it. When is it, the eighteenth? We'll go out. Just the two of us. You won't have to think about it at all."

The letter I threw away, but the stamp I cut off the envelope to save: a tiny portrait of a cross and a loop of thorns. It went under my bed, into the box that held my baby teeth, various notes from girls at school. All the sentimental moments of my life carefully hidden from my mother, taken out only in the darkness of my room, and one-by-one sifted through by candlelight.

When I finally got up the courage, I turned the engine over, and noticed that one of the headlights was out. I rummaged in the glove box for a new one, thinking I shouldn't drive in the snow without it, but found that the only one I had was broken; smashed in the packaging like a body in a coffin. It was the excuse I'd been looking for: It wasn't safe to go now. I might crash and die and one of the orderlies would tell him that it happened when I was on my way to see him and he would either cry over my body for the rest of his short life or simply not give a damn. Neither was what I wanted. On the phone, they said he only had a few conscious hours a day, and even then, he didn't say much. They could say I'd shown up while he slept. Tell him I left before he woke up. He would never know. I restarted my car and drove into town at a crawl.

I'm not sure how they found me. He had no way of knowing where I lived, and had they called my mother, I'm sure she would have told them many things, none of which would have been my phone number. I had few friends, and none of them knew about him. I'd told everyone he'd died when I was young: farming accident, arm caught in the machinery. The girl without a father. It always sounded good to me.

The nurse at the intake desk was large and deflated and not in a good mood.

"Audrey Klein," I said. "I'm here to see my – Jeremiah Hunt."

She looked through me over the file in her hand.

"You family?"

"Yes. He's my father."

She gave me the room number. I followed the signs up flights of stairs, down long, emotionless hallways. I crept along the tile floors, my hand trailing behind me on the waist-high bar that lined the walls. It caught here and there on the metal trying to slow me down, as if to say *Alright, you had your fun.*

The curtains were closed. A lamp at the bedside was on. It glared about the small room, casting shadows.

My father had been tall. Not necessarily strong, but lean. Wiry. Born to the fields, raised on the land, married a city girl then drove her away. He had never been hunched or broken. He had never been proud.

He lay with his back to me, his face to the curtained window, body curled tight into a ball. His shirt had come up slightly, and the lamp's harsh light outlined the bones of his gaunt back in darkness. He looked so small.

"Daddy?"

Hospital sounds filtered in through the open door. The click of heels on tile floor, murmuring voices, a woman crying, far away. The steady beep of machines, counting heartbeats. The silence of those done counting.

I moved slowly to the other side of him. The pillow lay on the floor beside the bed, and I used it as a cushion for my knees. He had both hands under his cheek, palm to palm, as if in prayer. His eyes were half-lidded and empty. The chasm of years yawned between us.

"Mom wishes she could be here," I said. "She had to work, but she really wants to see you."

A second passed. In the silence, I searched for what was difficult about that moment, and decided that it was how little I felt. He moved his cracked lips, just slightly, and exhaled. I moved closer. He made no sound.

"Never thought I'd catch you this far into town," I said. I willed myself to smile, but my face refused.

His lips moved again, and I put my ear up to his mouth. His warm breath stale, the smell of an empty room.

"The lamp," he said, his voice a gurgle at the back of his throat. He inhaled sharply. "Too..."

I waited for more, but nothing came. I laughed to prompt him further, to push him toward the memory, but it was like it had never happened. Light burned bright from the bedside table. He simply wanted the room to go dark.

It's a strange feeling, suddenly becoming a person without a past. Like being abandoned by gravity, having all your parts drift off in different directions, falling into the sky. Being erased by three words. Becoming nothing.

I moved around to the bedside table and studied the lamp as long as I could stand, then grabbed the switch and shut it off. The room went gray. I turned back to look at my father, but saw only the ghostly blue forms of light bulbs swimming in my vision. I moved for the door.

But I couldn't leave. It was still there, standing next to him like nothing had happened. Like It didn't know. I turned back, picked up the lamp. It was light, no more than a few pounds, just a stick of metal with a bulb on top, a shade the same color as the walls. Still, it could have done damage if swung. The base was weighted enough to hurt. I looked down at what was left of my father, lying like a clenched fist on the bed. How long had he been here like this? How much longer would he last?

I wrapped my hand around the darkened bulb. My body didn't realize it was being burned until I had already given the bulb two full twists, trying to pry it loose. White lights popped behind my eyes like camera flashes, and my hand snapped back on its own orders. But the bulb was still there, at the end of that sick, a few twists from freedom. My muscles suddenly alive, I brought the bulb down on the side table in one ungraceful movement, the sound of it tearing a hole in me. The next three whacks reduced it to nothing, left a dent in the wood. I had done it. The lamp was out.

In minutes, a nurse was rushing through the door, drawn by the sound of breaking glass. But I was already gone, rushing through the hallways and out the front door, into my car, down the highway, cradling my burned and blistered hand in my lap. It wasn't until I had made it all the way home—locked safely in my apartment, crouching on the bathroom floor—that I peeled away the blisters, shedding the skin to reveal the curious new flesh underneath.

"But where does He plug it in?" I asked my father, looking up into his face. Out across the valley, the sun was slowly crawling down below the hills, the glowing bulb clinging to the horizon like a drop of dew. His hand surrounded mine completely, and I felt so small, like I could curl up in his palm and drift away. I could feel the vibrations of his arm as he laughed.

"Plug it in?" he said, looking down at me. His smile was warm and golden, the color of cornfields and setting sunlight. "What makes you think He's got to plug it in? He's the power and the glory forever, amen!"

He flung his arms out wide, releasing my hand in the process. I let it hang limp at my side and stared at his shadow in the dirt laid out behind him. In the daylight, the fields after harvest looked barren and dull, covered in the butchered stumps of grain stalks, the dusty yellow of summer's end.

"Daddy, I want to stay here. With you."

His hand dropped back to his side and I reached out, my own small fist seeking refuge once again in the blanket of his palm. I'd be starting school soon. A new school, in a city, somewhere else. Away.

"No ma'am," he said, his mouth barely moving, "He doesn't need a plug or a cord or none of that. None of that stuff we need. He wants it done, all He has to do is speak it, and it's done, no matter what it is. Whether or not – "

He cleared his throat, then coughed. I inched sideways until my arm touched his thigh. I leaned into him and pictured myself fusing to his leg like an iron-on patch—indivisible.

"You know how many light bulbs it would take to shine that bright?" he said. "A zillion. Heck, probably a million zillion. How do you suppose He'd light up that many light bulbs? Ain't enough plugs in the world."

His arm was shaking again and I looked up. A few stars had poked through the sky, the sun no longer hiding them from sight. A tear clung to his cheek beside the fold of his nostril, filled with the last rays streaming out across the valley, a golden orb on his wrinkled face.

"With love?" I said.

His hand left mine again to wipe his face. He knelt down in front of me, his back to the last of the daylight. I squinted down into his silhouette.

"You're a bright girl, you know that," he said and smiled. I stared into the cracks between his crooked teeth. "A very bright girl."

He touched his hand to my cheek. I felt the wetness of his palm.

The power and the glory forever.

Amen.

Adam Dove is an author and editor born and living in Pittsburgh, PA. His short stories have appeared in a number of journals, including Asymmetry, Write Out, Every Day Fiction, and Open Minds Quarterly. His work addresses themes of personal identity, masculinity, and mental health in often strange and magical ways.

2

Six Degrees of Kevin Bacon by Katie Tarbell

Natalie Portman was in *Closer* with Clive Owen. Who was in *Children of Men* with Julianne Moore. Who was in *Crazy, Stupid, Love* with Kevin Bacon.

I take a deep breath, the tears pushed back for now as I stare down at the box in my hand. How would I describe the color? It's not pink, but not purple. It's too dull to be magenta. Perhaps it fits into the red category. Is it maroon? Maybe burgundy. I sit here for what feels like forever, focusing on the color. If focus on that, maybe I can forget that this is all that is left of my dad.

The car is silent as we drive back from the funeral home. It's been a few days since his funeral, but it still doesn't feel real. It feels like a movie, and any moment now he's going to walk into the room again like nothing ever happened.

You know, it's funny, as a kid, I used to hate when car rides were silent. When there was no sound, it usually meant my family was fighting, and the silence was always filled with a tension so thick it felt like it could suffocate me. Now, in the most awkward silence in my life, I think I'd be pissed if somebody started talking.

Mom finally pulls into the driveway and turns off the car. She doesn't hesitate to get out; neither does Sarah. My hands start shaking. I have to take off my seatbelt, open the door, step out of the car, walk into the house, and put dad down. At any point in that excursion, I could trip, fall, and drop him. And what if I do that? Will the lid on the box pop open?

What if his ashes get blown away by the wind? Is that how we scatter his ashes? In the front yard of this crappy apartment that he *never* lived in? This is too much responsibility; I'm not able to handle it.

The car door swings open, ripping me from my panicked thought. I jump, hugging the box even closer to my chest, so it doesn't fall.

Sarah is standing there with her arms outstretched to take the box from me, and I sigh in relief. I don't have to be the one to carry him inside. My sister saved me. I hand the box over as gently as possible. Sarah holds him tight to her chest and walks slowly into the house.

"Are you hungry?" Mom asks as she drops her purse onto the floor next to the kitchen table. "We could order subs."

My stomach clenches at the thought. "I'm not really hungry," I say. Mom stares at me blankly, even though I know what she's thinking. I haven't really been eating lately. It's not a big deal; I'm just not hungry. I'd say that's a fairly normal reaction, considering the circumstances.

"Well, do you want to stay for a while, or do you want to get home?"

I look over at Sarah, once again asking her to make the decision for me. All I want is to crawl into bed and not get up for the next month, and we can do that at our own apartment or here, I don't really care either way.

"We should probably get home," Sarah answers. "It's getting late, and I have work in the morning."

"Are you sure? You guys can stay over for a couple days if you want."

We should stay. Mom would be alone, and that's not fair to her. She and dad haven't been together for fifteen years, they've been apart longer than they were ever together, but I know that they still loved each other, even though they couldn't live together, that fact never stopped being true.

But I gave up my chance to make a decision. I gave it to Sarah, and she chose to go home. So we once again left our mother to go back to our apartment.

We don't live far away from mom, but it's not exactly an enjoyable trip. Sarah reaches over and grips my hand tightly when we pass by the hospital where he died.

Goldie Hawn was in *Death Becomes Her* with Meryl Streep. Who was in *The River Wild* with Kevin Bacon.

My mind won't stop replaying that day. If I let my thoughts wander freely, they inevitably wind up back in that hospital room, with the incessant beeping from the crash cart as the only sound I could focus on. I've been having a hard time getting it to focus on one thing. So far, the only thing that's been working is Six Degrees of Kevin Bacon. It takes a while to work through everyone's filmography to find the correct overlap. All that time, I can force my thoughts away from that moment, and that day.

"I want to move to the Rez," I blurt out at (what feels like) random.

"Oh yeah? Do you know what you would do for work?"

I shrug, my shoulders starting to slump. "I could work for the casino, or something."

"Did you talk to anyone while we were up there to see if you could stay with 'em?"

"No, I mean, I haven't made any solid decisions yet, I'm just thinking about it now." 'Course, I'm always just thinking of it, I have so many plans that will lead me to having a fantastic future. Yet I never do them. Why would this be any different?

"I think you should. It would be good for you."

My head jerks over to my sister in surprise. "Really?"

"Yeah, why not? They're your family too."

Huh. "Mom got angry when I told her that." I'd told her I wanted to live on the Rez for a year, as we were taking a walk during the wake. Since dad died, I decided I wanted to get to know his community more. I got the standard "What would you do about work" question, as well as a bunch of arguments about how stupid my idea was and how I don't really belong there. I dropped the subject not long after. It shouldn't surprise me that Sarah would have a different opinion than my mom, but it still does.

My mom is white, but my father is – *was* – Mohawk. She doesn't really like to acknowledge that a lot. I don't think it's for racist reasons, more that she hates that there's a large part of us that isn't her, I guess. Every time I would point out, "I'm Mohawk," "I'm Native," or any acknowledgement that I wasn't white, she would roll her eyes and snap "You're not *just* Mohawk, ya know!" After a while I just stopped acknowledging it at all, instead choosing to be neither white, nor Mohawk, and just be Quinn.

I wonder if my dad died thinking I was ashamed to be Indian.

The tears start falling again, but I try to wipe them away quickly. I don't want Sarah to see me cry again. I ask too much of her as it is.

Shirley Temple was in *The Bachelor and the Bobby-Soxer* with Cary Grant. Who was in *Arsenic and Old Lace* with Jack Carson. Who was in *Cat on a Hot Tin Roof* with Paul Newman. Who was in *Road to Perdition* with Tom Hanks. Who was in *Apollo 13* with Kevin Bacon.

The rest of the trip home is once again in silence. Up in the apartment, Sarah immediately heads into her room, while I make a beeline for mine. From inside my night stand, I pull out a pipe, a grinder, and a glass jar. Tonight is not a night to remain sober.

I lean back against my pillows and take my first hit, holding the smoke into my lungs as long as possible.

I watched my dad die. That's something I didn't think I would experience at my age. I'm not a child, granted, but I'm still in my early twenties. I'm not ready to be without a dad yet. Yet here I am. With what's left of my father fitting in a tiny reddish purplish box.

I probably won't end up moving to the Rez.

Katie Tarbell has been coming up with stories since she was old enough to think coherent thoughts. She received a Bachelor's Degree in English from the University at Buffalo in 2012, and has been working at trying to get her stories out there ever since. The story included in this anthology is based off her feelings following the death of her own father and what it means to be Mohawk. She currently resides in Buffalo.

3

Austin Daniels is Dead by Chris Elliott

Immediately after death, there is a state that is referred to among the dead as "dead dead." Dead dead is dead, make no mistake about that, but people who are dead dead can still observe people who are alive, an opportunity that gives the dead dead some real pleasure. The dead dead can visit other people's lives, though only to the degree that the living remained interested in them. That's how it works. The dead dead can see into the lives of people they've known, or people who know of the dead dead person through anecdote or fame, but only as long as someone who is alive continues to think of them. And it can't be just one person accidentally running into some obscure tangential reference during a microfilm search at a library either. It has to be people who loved or admired the person. With most people, the only people who love them know them. It's not always the case, but usually it is.

One passionate person could certainly keep a dead person dead dead for a long time, but it's a combination of quality and quantity that the dead dead quickly recognize as their only hope for awareness. Birthdays were always good.

The thoughts on earth of the dead dead person must be positive for there to be any elevation of their compromised consciousness. Hateful remembrances shed no light. Only longing, fondness, respect, admiration and laughter can pierce the membrane between dead dead and gone. Once the dead dead's last remaining positive spiritual contact with the living is gone, so are they. For the dead dead, being in the thoughts of a person still alive is their only lifeline.

The newly dead dead are usually quite busy. Immediately after a person is dead, he or she is spoken of frequently, and the newly dead dead's consciousness is transported to a window of light and mind that can dance across the world.

But that slows down quickly, then lingers, then disappears. It is common for anyone who dies young and active to be dead dead for sixty years or more, and in that way, they are among the most fortunate of all the suspended souls. The vigor of the dead dead's relative consciousness varies directly with the frequency and intensity of the living's remembrance of them, so for nearly all of the dead dead, the last few years are bleak and dreary.

Of course, some people are never forgotten; great leaders, thinkers and artists live forever through their works and deeds, and there is a mechanism in place to accommodate such greatness. Such persons are graduated to the death hall of fame after one hundred years of remaining in the minds of the living. Hall of Fame membership is reviewed centennially and members are often removed.

By the end of a common person's run of being dead dead, though, there isn't much light left. The dead dead's only earthly remembrance is the occasional thought from a son or a daughter, now also soon to be dead. By the time the dead dead's life light is like a single candle, the end is usually welcome. When a month passes without the dead dead being thought of by anyone who is alive, the dead dead dies, and enters death's final stage, which is called dead dead dead.

Though extremely difficult, there is a way to get out of being dead dead dead. On a sliding scale relative to the length of time a person has been dead dead dead, given a sufficient worldly clamor for the decedent's remembrance, dead dead dead status could be rolled back to dead dead, and that is precisely what happened to Austin Daniels.

Austin Daniels was one of the busiest men ever to be dead dead. Daniels was a legendary Tennessee whiskey maker who was killed in the Civil War, and as such he had remembrances from family and friends, as well as soldiers, citizens who had heard surely overtold stories of his heroism, but mostly, he was known for his skills in distilling. People would drive their wagon trains from Georgia north and Kentucky south to buy him out of his clear White Lightning and his barrel-aged Rye.

"You think of me when your work is done and you're sipping my whiskey," he would say when he sold a case to a man recently arrived on a wagon train. "My name is on every bottle. Look at my name when you drink that whiskey and thank me personally. You thank me!" Austin Daniels was a noisy, chest-thumping, good-ol'-boy with long, curling blonde hair and a handlebar moustache that was almost red. His ruddy, slightly pocked, sanguine complexion contrasted fierce blue eyes, and his voice rose above all others in a loud room of men drinking.

When he joined to go to war, he assured his captain, "I'll kill more Yanks in a month than your next best man in two!" And he fulfilled his challenge to himself with heroism and bravery that far exceeded his duty and his brag.

He took a ball in the chest at Gettysburg, and as he lay dying, he spoke to his captain. "They're going to make statues out of me. You just watch. The south is never going to forget Austin Daniels!"

As high an opinion as he had of himself, his opinion of others was just as low. Wildly suspicious of even the closest associates of the distillery, he never wrote down his recipe for barrel-aged Rye, and he organized the flow of labor so that no single employee was privy to even a third of the total process.

When a young man dies a war hero and carries the legend of his liquor to the grave, it is news in Dixie. The day of Austin Daniels' death he was the talk of the south. There was an enormous funeral at which he was eulogized by General Lee; there were women crying, and men had fights over how unfair it was for him to have died so young and violently. Men would agree with one another that it was a terrible thing fate had brought to Austin Daniels, but for some reason, they would fight anyway.

A year after his death, a movement stirred to declare the anniversary of his passing a state holiday, but the movement withered as the war grew more and more horrible, and that's when the slide in his afterlife started. In Austin Daniel's first year of his death, he was the envy of the dead

dead, conscious practically all the time, going back home to Tennessee, all over the rest of the south, up to New England, and even to California, sometimes to Europe, Australia, and even Asia.

About five years after his passing, he had occasional down time for the first time in his death death, and frankly, Austin Daniels didn't mind it. Being everywhere all the time was tiring, and he welcomed the occasional lapses of stimulation. This second stage of death death was also very kind to Daniels. His brew was a seven-year barrel-aged Rye, and he had the unique advantage over every other young dead dead person he knew in releasing a hundred barrels of whiskey once a year for the next seven years. That is a thing that will keep you on people's minds.

Even relatively celebrated people drop out of dead dead and into dead dead dead faster than the recently deceased ever imagine they will. At the time of death, many gather around the dying, so the newly dead feel relevant to life at the moment of crossing over. In a manner of thinking, death is barely perceptible to the newly dead, dead dead being eerily similar to life relative to life's lack of interest in the living's final years, months and moments. The dead dead also soon learn how quickly they are forgotten, and how infrequently they are remembered. To his discredit, Austin Daniels watched with glee as some of the most famous dead dead people that had entered death death at around the same time he did faded into the blackness of death death death.

In the eighth year after Austin Daniel's death, there was a big drop, both in the brightness of the light around him, and in the frequency with which it shone. The Austin Daniels distillery continued to make whiskey, but it was not nearly as good as the spirits that came from his own hand. His name was still on the bottle, but people did not like the whiskey nearly as well, and sales dropped off dramatically. The distillery went bankrupt not a dozen years past his passing, and before long, drinkers turned their fancy toward other formerly inferior distillers.

Despite his battlefield heroics, Austin Daniels' holiday was never named, and no statue was ever erected. Austin Daniels went from being a southern icon to just another dead soldier, hoping for someone, anyone to lend him a thought or a word. He had had no children, so while his light burned bright and hot early, he was disadvantaged relative to many of his dead dead peers in terms of longevity. His attitude toward the dimming of the light of others had been such that among the dead dead, there was little sympathy for the ebb of Austin Daniels' effulgence.

It had been twenty years since his fatal wound at Gettysburg, and his remembrance had dwindled to the occasional random flicker across the mind of a senile old man whose life he had saved on the battlefield, or an old drunk, whose life had been destroyed by his discovery of Austin Daniels' barrel-aged Rye. On the day that a single lumen of light shone up at him from the darkness, Austin Daniels knew the end was near. Its steady glow lasted a month, and then went out.

***

That was the last thing Austin Daniels remembered until he was ripped out of being dead dead dead by what felt like the hands of a giant. He was suddenly floating in a huge, bustling convention center, and a man on the stage spoke from an oaken lectern. Next to the lectern was a table, and on the table was a glass case that contained what looked to Austin to be a bottle of his barrel-aged Rye. The man on the stage spoke.

"Austin Daniels was said to have made the finest whiskey in the south. When he was killed at the Battle of Gettysburg one hundred and forty years ago, his recipe died with him. This is an authenticated bottle from the last batch of Austin Daniels whiskey ever to leave the distillery while he was still in charge. The bottle was a gift to a friend of Daniels, and the label is signed, along with a note that reads 'Think of me when you drink this. Yours in friendship, Austin Daniels.' We'll start the bidding at five-hundred dollars."

A pale, thin man in a dark suit held up a blue paddle.

"Six hundred," the auctioneer said. A stubble-bearded man in jeans and a white tee shirt held up his hand.

"Seven hundred." A red paddle across the room went up.

"A thousand!" shouted the man in jeans.

"Eleven hundred?" the auctioneer queried. The blue paddle again.

"Twelve hundred," the auctioneer said. The man in jeans raised his hand again.

"Thirteen hundred." Blue paddle.

"Fourteen hundred." Hand.

"Fifteen hundred." No paddle, red or blue. "Fifteen hundred once...fifteen hundred twice...sold to the gentleman for fourteen hundred dollars."

Two other men flanked the winning bidder in congratulations, one a casually dressed white man with dreadlocks to his waist and the other a short, cheerful black man who spoke in a light Jamaican accent. "You win, Jimmy mon, you win. You know I tink you crazy, but you win."

The white dred said, "Jimmy likes what Jimmy likes, and if he has the money, he can spend it however he wants."

Austin floated over to the auctioneer and clucked with pride. "You're damn right I made the best whiskey in the south." He floated through the air, following the three back to the parking lot. They drove from the auction house in what Austin quickly figured out was the city of Boston, up I-95 to a rented house in the South end of Portsmouth, New Hampshire, Daniels all the while marveling at the horseless buggies that spangled the road. He was the topic of conversation all the way home, a thing he adored above all else, and he had an invisible seat on the dashboard from which to observe it.

When they arrived at the house, a tall pretty girl in her early twenties dressed in antique clothing that a city girl might have worn back when he was alive was painting the inside hallway.

"Hey Jeanie!" the white dred said.

"Hey Joel! Chester! Jimmy, what happened?" The pretty blond laid the paint roller down in the paint tray and with her wrist brushed a dangling forelock over her ear.

"I did it! I went and did it," Jimmy said.

"How much?"

"Fourteen hundred dollars."

"Oh my God! Jimmy, that's just crazy."

"Das what I tol' him too, Jeanie..." Chester, the smiley Jamaican, said.

Jimmy continued. "And just in time for the Friday Fine Spirits Club. As soon as Chris gets here – "

Right on cue a man in his early forties, who had obviously been a handsome fellow earlier in his life, but whose potbelly and strange and unflattering balding patterns had left him with a disquieting appearance. "Jimmy, what did you do?"

"What do you think I did? I bought it. Fourteen hundred bucks for one bottle of one-hundred-forty-year-old barrel-aged Rye whiskey, signed by Austin Daniels himself. And you're just in time to help us taste it."

"Jimmy, you can't drink that whiskey. It's a historical document. That would be like screwing a mummy!"

"Chris, I figure I could get hit by a car as soon as I leave this house, and then where would I be?"

Austin Daniels had some wisdom on that subject, but he knew he would be unable to clue Jimmy in. He agreed with Jimmy, though, and shouted to no one who could hear him, "Jimmy's right, Chris! Drink the whiskey!"

Jimmy peeled the paper off the top of the bottle and popped the cork before Chris could say another word. "Too late," he said.

Jimmy filled five short shot glasses with the sparkling amber liquid and set a glass in front of Jeanie and the four men. They sniffed, swirled, and then sipped the whiskey and a silence fell upon the room. Jeanie was first to speak. "Oh my God."

"Holy – "

"This is – "

"Das de bes' ting I ever tasted, mon."

"Wow."

Jimmy proposed a toast. "To Austin Daniels."

The other four said together, "To Austin Daniels!"

Austin Daniels hovered in the air above them and couldn't recall ever having felt warmer or more bathed in light, even in the days and weeks immediately following his death. There was something more delicious about fond remembrance from strangers across the ages than even close friends from his own lifetime.

They finished the bottle over the course of the next convocation of the Portsmouth Friday Fine Spirits Club, and Austin Daniels' spirit hovered above and within each one. Jimmy corked the empty bottle and set it on the top shelf of the liquor cabinet, and as he closed the door and the last shafts of light from the kitchen disappeared, Austin Daniels too slipped into darkness.

Chris Elliott is a writer and musician living in Los Angeles, most recently employed as a copywriter for the world's largest musical instrument retailer in its band and orchestra division. His deep knowledge of jazz, blues and popular music, as well as his quick wit has made him an ideal pick as the chief interviewer for Woodwind & Brasswind, the largest online band and orchestra retailer. In 2019, he co-wrote, produced and co-starred in "Somebody Dies," two one-act plays directed by and starring Tony-winning actor Kent Klineman at The Players' Ring Theatre in Portsmouth, NH. He has recently completed work on a musical.

Chris's trumpet is never far from his side. He is the trumpet player and horn arranger for The Tribe, a band of professional musicians who organize benefit shows for LA charities featuring such well-known vocal artists as David Crosby, Lisa Loeb, Al Jardine and many others. In 2007, his series of dispatches from a weeklong musical engagement in Baghdad's Green Zone ran as a centerpiece in the Sunday Boston Globe.

He is uniquely versatile musician, stand-up comedian, spoken word artist and storyteller with an inspired command of music, writing and live performance. Chris holds a B.A. in English from Yale University.

4

I Was Born in Nineteen Seventy ... Whatever by Sybil Wilen

"Listen, I have to tell you something."

I almost hung up the phone then because I just didn't want to hear it. I mean, I knew it already, I knew it in the tone of his voice, but in reality I knew it in his posture – and in his eyes that no longer met mine. I knew it in the distance between calls. And there was the fact that I hadn't seen him in over a month. Most importantly, our sex life had stopped abruptly that night nine months ago.

"I don't want to hear it," I said. There I was being all polite. Isn't that what had gotten me where I was? Being nice – being agreeable. I was always trying to keep the peace when everyone was angry about something.

And everyone was angry about the lack of jobs, the lack of housing, the lack of anything to do – angry about just life.

"It's just that I've been thinking."

"Of course you have." My tongue felt venomous. I rolled my eyes and considered laying the phone in its cradle and pulling the plug from the wall. Let him keep talking into a vast nothingness. That's what it all felt like anyway. Like we were circling in space and whatever it all was meant to be about was consistently being vacuumed away.

I looked down at my twenty-three-month-old baby, Arlo, asleep next to me. His mouth was opened slightly and the blanket beneath his head was wet from his sleep sweats. I stared down at my expanding stomach. Tomorrow I would find out if my little guy's brother was going to have to be evicted. He seemed reluctant to make his appearance. Who could blame him? There wasn't much to be coming out to. A single mother, an older brother. No one else in the world who would give a damn about him and I wasn't even certain what my thoughts were regarding him. I had a lot to think about at the moment. I had arrangements dangling in the shadows on who was going to take care of Arlo if I had to give birth. I really didn't have time for this shit.

"I know what you want to say." I waited a beat, but there was no response. "We broke up ages ago, Todd. You might not have said it officially, but I knew. You knew. Fuck, everyone knows!" I wished I had a cigarette. I know, I know. Everyone shakes their head at smoking pregnant women. Yes, it was 1992 and everyone knew better. Yadda, yadda, yadda. I wasn't going to have one. But – I really fucking wanted one.

There was silence on the other end. Was Todd hanging up? I listened for a click. Then I heard him clear his throat. No dice. He was still there.

"I know I shouldn't have pushed you to go to trial." His voice was hollow.

I sighed. No, he shouldn't have – but my usual side was climbing through me. I longed to tell him it was okay, that everything was okay. It didn't matter. I was doing well despite everything. I bit my lip to keep from talking.

"I really should have stayed out of it."

"I could have told you what would happen. I wasn't surprised by the verdict." There, that was some kind of compromise. I didn't totally sound like a chump.

"Well, I've been thinking about it for awhile." Oh, I bet you have. I was pretty certain what happened to me went through his mind over and over again when he was with that little redhead I had seen him around Seattle with.

"I think I should tell you what I've realized in person," he said. I closed my eyes and tried to push the thoughts from my mind. I saw a fist. I saw the cigarette butt in the grass. I saw my wrist bent at an odd angle and the red and gray plaid flannel swam into watery view.

"I'd rather you not." I could hear music blaring – loud and rushing through my head. I remembered what song was playing and I never ever wanted to hear Soundgarden again.

"I think I thought – "

"You think you thought? What does that even mean?" My throat was dry and my voice sounded raspy.

"Okay, okay. I thought if there was a conviction that it would somehow make me feel better. Make it good. No, that's the wrong word. I'm sorry. I rehearsed this before I called and I still can't get it fucking right."

"Did you write it down?"

"What?"

"What you wanted to say."

"No, I didn't think of that."

"Then, I guess you'll just have to wing it."

He went silent. I looked around the small room. I had managed to get a bed from a friend's mom who felt bad for me. The table next to me was a milk crate with a scarf over it. I had a chest of drawers from a yard sale. That was a good catch. It set me back three dollars that I almost didn't spend because that could buy milk for Arlo or cigarettes for me. I was glad in the end when I found a twenty dollar bill curled up in the back of the top drawer.

Arlo's grandparents had each donated items specifically for him. They didn't care for their son anymore, had disowned him eight years before when he was sixteen by kicking him out of each of their houses respectively. They didn't care much for each other as well having divorced seven years before that. That was such a theme of my childhood. Parents divorcing, parents not wanting to be burdened with raising the offspring of their mating, parents kicking their kids out. I guess the eighties was a time, not only of great excess for some, but great independence as well. Independence from responsibilities. It seemed like our entire generation was made up of unwanted children who infringed upon our parent's desire to turn on, tune in, and drop out. Screw that Generation X, Slacker shit. We were Generation Unloved, Unwanted. We were Generation Whatever.

When I was fifteen suffering through biology class, I learned that fair hair and blue eyes were recessive genes and that if two people with these traits came together and reproduced, their children would be blond with blue eyes as well. This struck me because my parents and younger siblings all shared these traits. With my dark brown hair, brown eyes, and permanent tan, I didn't. It never seemed like a big deal, but there I was learning that dark hair and eyes were dominant traits and that if someone dark made children with someone fair, chances were good that their children would be dark, though like most things biologically, there were exceptions.

I made an ass out myself in class by telling the teacher she was full of shit because I was living proof that two fair people could have a dark child. She didn't argue with me, but I could tell from her expression that something was up. I immediately pinned my mom down after she got home from work and after some questions and then a lot of screaming back and forth, I learned that I was apparently fathered by some strung-out hippie back in the early seventies who my mother met on her journey to find herself in California.

Not too long after that, I ran away. I don't know why, really. No one ever mistreated me at home – but they definitely always seemed "off", the more and more I thought about it. We lived in a decent little town in Western Massachusetts. I had nice things. But, I couldn't help scrutinizing how my little brother (half) and sister (half) were my parents' 100% children. I remembered my parents talking about following the Grateful Dead and they would sometimes talk about how I was with them when they did so, but I didn't remember anything too far back from my brother's (half) birth in the early 80's.

Sometimes I would catch myself muttering, "I hate my life, I hate my life" over and over under my breath.

My mother often reminded me of all the things she could have been had she not had us kids. An artist, a writer, a rock star, a fucking debutante. Whatever suited her need at the moment. She'd narrow her eyes at me and gesture with her cigarette like she wanted badly to poke me in the chest with it to make her point. Oh, right, and she couldn't abort me because I came along before Roe V Wade. Fuck that. I could have exercised that right when I found out I was pregnant the first time – but I believed I had found my forever mate in Jeremy and that our child would be full of unconditional love.

Of course, I still had plenty of time to terminate when Jeremy dumped my ass before I got to announce our imminent parenthood.

I had come back from the clinic ready to tell him the news to find someone had taken my place in his eyes and in my bed. I say my bed because it literally was mine. As was the rest of the furniture. Not to mention that the apartment was in my name because I paid for that, too. I had a day job schlepping coffee and a night job stocking shelves. Jeremy was going to be a rock star.

After I got over my shock, I tried to tell Jeremy what was going on, but as soon as the words were out, my replacement hauled off and punched me in the stomach. She pulled her arm back for a second jab, but I ran for the door before she made contact. Jeremy got in the way and pushed me. He had never so much as raised his voice at me, so this caught me off-guard and I froze, unsure what to do next.

"Grab her, grab her," the apple of his eye called, but he only made a half-hearted attempt and I bolted, leaving them my belongings and the apartment.

A few days later, with the help of Jeremy's mother, I did manage to contact the landlord, who always liked me. He removed my name from the lease and told me not to worry about the rest.

At that point, I moved in with a girl band. They had plans to take over the music industry with their raw, angry feminism. They cooed and cawed over me and tried to talk me into getting an abortion. But, for whatever reason, I just couldn't bring myself to do so.

I didn't really understand my resistance. I was pro-choice. I had thought I would have been a good abortion candidate upon finding out the story behind my existence. But, night after night, I found myself whispering to my baby that his life would be different. That I would never lie to him. He would grow up in truth. And almost three years later, I was looking at the same choice after that fucking concert. And I was stuck in the same place. I just couldn't walk through that mob in front of the clinic and open that door.

"I fucking hate my life," I uttered, rubbing my belly.

"What?" Todd was still on the phone. I cradled the receiver on my shoulder.

"Nothing."

"Are you mad at me?"

"What?"

"Mad, angry, disappointed, pissed?"

Why was he still on the phone? "I don't know."

"I would be."

"That's nice to know." I was worried I might start humming. That was something I did when I was feeling anxious or angry.

"I'm mad at me."

I sighed.

"What do you want me to say, Todd?"

"Nothing. I want you to hear me out."

"So speak."

"I just realize that I wanted you to press charges for me, not you. I didn't really have your needs at heart."

"I don't really want to talk about it anymore."

"I know. I know it was wrong to keep asking you what happened and putting you through all of that ordeal."

I sighed heavily and Arlo shifted in his sleep. I laid my hand on his chest and looked down at his baby cheeks and wispy blond hair. I thought about how he carried Jeremy's last name and that Jeremy had chosen his first name. I carried him in my body and was raising him on my own and yet, we would forever be separated by names. I thought about the first time Jeremy held him, he turned to me and said, "I feel nothing for him." And my replacement giggled, her hand rising to her scarlet-painted lips.

Somewhere in all of this mess, I longed to feel like a feminist, but every move I made put me under some guy.

"We weren't together very long, Todd. Don't worry about it."

"I'm not talking about us. I knew we weren't a thing."

"Well, I guess we just had a thing."

"Stop it, Stephanie." I cringed. I still wasn't used to that name. I wasn't really sure why I chose it when I ran away. I guess I wanted a more normal-sounding name than the one I grew up with. Who names their kid, Mable these days? Able Mable. Maybe Mable. For Christ's sake, my mother told everyone my name was a family name, but my grandmother informed me of the truth. Mabel was the name of the tortoiseshell cat my mother had grown up with. I was named after the fucking family pet. And my mother couldn't even spell it correctly. I shook my head.

"Todd, I've got to go. It's been really nice talking to you, but Arlo is napping and I want some time to myself before he wakes up."

"Are you really round now?"

"What?"

"How full are you? You're at the end, right?"

"Jesus fucking Christ. I'm hanging up now."

"Wait, Steph – hear me out."

"Why? You've got a problem, Todd. If you like pregnant girls so much, knock up that pig nose chick you've been running around with." And like that, I found my feminism and hung up the fucking phone.

Sybil Wilen's debut short story collection, Now Look What You've Done was published in 2012, followed by Love Sutra: A Collection of Flash Fiction. Her short stories have appeared in Night Picnic Journal, Burnt Pine Magazine, Dark Sky, The Baltimore Review, Words & Images, Solstice Magazine, & Images, and in the anthologies The New Dead, Haunted M.E., Lovecraft M.E., Spirits of Yuletide, and Haunted Love. She has published articles in Carpe Nocturne, Middle Eastern Dance in New England, Casco Bay/Maine Weekly, and anthologies by Llewellyn World Wide. She lives in Maine with her family.

5

Four Poems From Remains by Heather Richmond

Heaven

My daughter asks where we go when we die
I answer Google
I say when we die, we live on in the memories of those who loved us
but then they realize they don't know nearly enough about us
so they frantically type our names into Google
and maybe even the genealogy sites if they're fancy like that.
And they search and they search
hoping some search engine will tell them
why the car made that fateful turn, or how long the cancer was growing
before it was detected
and how we felt on the first day of school
and what our relationship was like with our father.
And if they're lucky, they'll find a clue
they can add like a prized possession to their memories of us.
And that's where we live, in those clues in the cloud
when we die

Spring

Spring is an ominous event
this year:
the grackles and the tennis matches and the
three-legged cat hold dubious charm.
We don't even notice the magnolias
until their petals litter
the street like the neighbor's trash.
Maybe it's those clouds,
the ones that always storm elsewhere,
but even the fat man holding a basketball hoop
in back of a speeding pickup
makes me wish for snow.

Still

Even after it happened, still we sat on soft carpet
in front of the fire while our perfect little girl played around us.
Even after it happened we ate those big Southern meals that your
father cooks,
his hair grown back after the successful chemotherapy.
Even after it happened, the trees bloomed and the blooms stayed
despite the cold temperatures at night.
Even still.
So my hand still wants to find its way to the place on your belly
where our secret was
so our girl still plays babies like we were wanted her to
so those clothes still hang in the closet like ghosts of the future.
Even still.
It's not so bad.

Mathematician

He held a cigarette;
it was the 1950s.
He held it too long, too
close to the page;
comtemplating,
note-taking,
sketching equations
in a darkening room.
Three years later,
sorting his life,
that singed moment clings to my thumb
and I sit, for a moment
comtemplating
cracked paper
and faded equations
in a darkening room.

Heather Richmond is an archivist, former bookseller, and secret poet. A native of Portland, Oregon, she has lived most of her adult life in the Midwest. She currently lives with her wife and daughter in Columbia, Missouri. She has a B.A. in Creative Writing from Beloit College, where she won the White-Howells English Prize in Poetry.

6

But I'm Famous Here by Kim Sedlock

Once upon a time, there were three very different musicians. There was an anonymous musician (whom we will actually refer to as The Anonymous Musician) – he played trombone and didn't really live anywhere in particular, although he happened to be passing through Cleveland. There was a famous musician named Drew Lawrence who played electric guitar, of course, and did not live anywhere in particular, either, although he owned many houses. And there was a neighborhood musician named Marvin who also played trombone but lived in an efficiency apartment in Cleveland. He had nothing in common at all with The Anonymous Musician, except that they both happened to play trombone and for a couple weeks, they were both in Cleveland. It's all too easy to get two trombone players mixed up with each other, but I assure you that all three of these musicians were extremely different people, from the bottom of their souls to the very tips of their fingers.

The Anonymous Musician sat in some coffee shop in Cleveland, humming to himself, oblivious of his surroundings. He scribbled on his napkin, drummed a little on the table, spontaneously wrote a whole new song, listening to the melody in his head, honoring the lyrics that seemed to be given to him, dictated to him from some invisible void that hovered just above his head, perhaps also created *by* his head. He wasn't sure and didn't care. He drank more coffee, beamed that he had a new song, one that would convey all the different dimensions of the word "transmission." He hunched over his trombone case and picked at the Greyhound sticker on it, still beaming.

There was physical transmission: how the spices one person adds to a soufflé land on another person's tongue and how their photo of their mom travels to other countries over the internet; mental transmission: how the thoughts of an eighteenth-century philosopher find an Alaskan school teacher and then through her, find a bored teenager; emotional transmission: how joy and tension are contagious in an office, at a party, in eager correspondence. Positive transmission, negative transmission – he found it all within that melody – a melody which seemed to find him, when all he was doing was staring out the window at an empty sidewalk being hit by a heavy rain. He shoved all the scribbled-on napkins into his pockets and tipped the barista a twenty. After all, she had brought the coffee that had kept him here creating during this storm. Without her, there would only be water, and then it might have been a whole different song.

The barista didn't see the twenty tucked under his cup until he was out of sight. She wanted to greet him by name the next time he came in, but realized she couldn't, because they hadn't exchanged names, although he had chattered about his bus ride and about how he loved the sound of the storm. For his first ten minutes there, in fact, he had seemed to be doing nothing but listening to it.

At the same time, several states away, Drew Lawrence stepped forward for his guitar solo. The lighting crew had changed where his spotlight happened for this arena stage, but he got into it and hit his groove, his energy peaked, the energy of thousands of onlookers fed him. He dropped to his knees in the jeans that the costume crew had torn for him and his fingers flew up and down his hundred-grand electric guitar. His sweat dripped down onto the guitar, mostly from the spotlight, and he shut his eyes. When he opened them, everyone was dancing and screaming, as far back as he could see, far back into the field in every direction, all their eyes were on him. He looked just the way he did in the poster – perfect bone structure, six-pack abs, and just the right amount of leather in his outfit. He jumped back to his feet and grinned his wild smile. There was no greater high than this.

A third musician, who was always just known as Marvin, sat on his stoop. He lived in a tiny neighborhood within a Cleveland ghetto. He didn't venture out of that tiny neighborhood much, except for work. To him, it was like a close-knit small town that happened to be situated in the midst of something larger than itself, but not necessarily greater than itself. He loved his stoop. He tuned his trombone on it every night around ten, and people would stop and chat with him. He knew so many of the people who walked down that street at night and he was happy to put down his instrument and talk with them. He wanted to hear about their days. Then he might pick up the old trombone and play some little ditty that they requested. There was no better way to spend an evening.

Meanwhile, around midnight that same night, The Anonymous Musician from the coffee shop could not sleep. He thought it was the coffee, but actually the barista had accidentally given him decaf for his order and for every refill. He was simply excited about his new song. He played it quietly near his window again and again and felt more peaceful than if he *had* slept.

The Anonymous Musician was crashing in Marvin's neighborhood indefinitely, just down the block from Marvin actually. But he didn't know or care.

Drew Lawrence returned to the stage from his dressing room, where the lights around his vanity mirror were almost as bright as the stage lights. He was followed by the costume crew who dressed him and redressed him quickly and accurately between acts and who wanted his current costume back. They walked a few feet behind him in circles, as he scoured the stage for his lucky bandana. It had been tied around his boot.

"We didn't want you to wear that, anyway," one of the costume crew snapped at him.

But he saw it around the wrist of someone in the lighting crew who was guzzling down some water, and he snatched it back. Then he ran to his dressing room again to meet up with security and get ushered out the door to the limo. He wore his photo face on his way out, and then opened a bottle of vodka in the back of the limo.

His entire band was in separate limos, all going to different places. He, unfortunately, was going home, and home was South Dakota, in a tiny house filled with Evangelists, where he was neither famous nor even considered a good person. He finished a quarter of the vodka bottle and checked his hands for hangnails. His fans and bandmates loved his calloused, beat-up, guitarist hands, but his mother hated any sign of hangnails. She would only forgive them if you were farming. "Hangnails are a sign of a slovenly attitude," she would say.

This would be his last limo for a week. When his stern, silent father met him at the airport, he would be in the family pick-up truck again, listening to the Christian news station and staring at flat farmland and forced into silence himself. They had no television, read no magazines, had no friends outside of their insulated church.

They didn't know that their least favorite son was famous. And, furthermore, they wouldn't really have cared. They knew he played rock music and that rock music ruined children's lives, and that was all they needed to know.

Around the same time that Drew Lawrence had been on a plane from Vegas to South Dakota, Marvin had been in a different part of Cleveland than his little neighborhood, staring at the clock on the office wall while his boss told him that he could learn to be better at filing with a little online tutoring. There were programs that taught more advanced systems of filing and then quizzed you about them, and apparently, these programs were free. What amazing luck for Marvin.

Most people his age had retired, but Marvin was a trombone-player. Two hours from now, he would be in his own neighborhood, walking into his own church for potluck supper, and everyone there knew him – he was THE trombone-player in his neighborhood. Everyone would want to sit with him, someone would pull out his chair, he would give autographs to little girls and grandmas alike, and when he took the stage in that church hall, it was silent.

For the people in his neighborhood, Marvin was the best they had ever seen live.

"After you get better with the new filing system," his boss continued, "we can work on your typing speed."

Meanwhile, The Anonymous Musician woke up and immediately put on some vinyl. Then he lay back down and just listened. It was going to be a great day. He thought he had passed a park near that coffee shop. It was going to be a very great day.

Drew Lawrence woke up in South Dakota. In that time zone, it was nine in the morning, which meant everyone else in the family had been up for four hours. He ate his oatmeal silently while his father sat at the table across from him and stared down at the rooster tablecloth. "When are you going to turn your life around and decide to make something of yourself?" his father said. One of his younger sisters ran by with his bandana tied around her doll's head. His mother was in the bedroom praying for him.

"I'm a famous guitarist," he told his father for the millionth time.

His father shook his head and told him to stop with the lies.

Drew Lawrence watched his teenage brother out the kitchen window, on his tractor. Maybe someday, my brother will "discover" me in a record store, Drew Lawrence thought and smiled.

His mother came out of the bedroom and stared at his hands. He had a new hangnail.

Drew Lawrence didn't last the entire week. He made a few calls and booked a driver to Minneapolis, a city he had never been in before. Less than an hour in downtown Minneapolis, though, and he was at a party in a fancy hotel with hordes of adoring fans he had never met before, yet who all had his lyrics memorized. He sang along with them and stared out the window at the city below.

Marvin lived alone in an efficiency apartment with a roach problem. He had lived in that same spot for most of his life. I have certainly sacrificed everything for my art, Marvin thought to himself, as he pulled his bed out from the couch. His church supper "gig" had ended an hour ago and would happen again next week. He couldn't sleep and he took his trombone out of its stickered-up case and sat on the edge of his bed with it and played an hour on his own.

All the while, there was something big that Marvin didn't know. You see, while Marvin was a good trombone-player for his church – and he was even a good trombone-player for his neighborhood – Marvin wasn't a good trombone-player. He was just okay.

Meanwhile, The Anonymous Musician put his case on the grass. He was already tuned-up, so he just started playing. With a great sense of euphoric release, he played for six hours without realizing it.

On his way out of the hotel, Drew Lawrence saw a fake Greek vase in the lobby that was the exact same type and colors as his parents owned: twice the size of an ordinary vase, formed like an angular hourglass, white and bright blue, depicting the Greek muses. It was something they had saved for and ordered from a catalogue. It had been around for most of his childhood, though. It had been filled with gaudy orange flowers at their Thanksgiving dinners when the men had sung the high school football songs and filled with a dozen long-stem red roses when his sister had her toddler ballet recital. That was back when he was one of them, when they could talk. He walked up to it and ran his hands over it and cried with no sound. The only thing he loved besides his family was being a rock star. But he had loved it so much that it had brought him into an entirely different world, one from which he couldn't exactly return – even when he did return. He could never really be present at their table anymore. His secret life was just too big to share with them. Anyway, they didn't want to know.

"Drew Lawrence!" a tiny pink-haired groupie shrieked and ran up to him.

"Hi," he said softly and tried to feel her love.

Marvin woke up to the alarm and dreaded going to his office job. He was a celebrity in his own neighborhood and yet those office people treated him like he was a loser. Today would be different, he vowed.

He had a tin drawer in his efficiency kitchen that was filled with all his schwag: recordings of all his music, gig posters, and a newspaper article clipping with his picture and a brief review. Today, he would bring all of it into the office and show it to them.

And he did. He showed it all to each of them a couple times, because he couldn't understand their silence. He didn't realize that they thought he was self-promoting and delusional.

Drew Lawrence went back to work, too. He felt at home again when he was centerstage. He felt fully himself and known. Everything he thought and felt and did and experienced was shared with a million people he had never met before. He reached his hand into the ray of the stage light and tried to grasp it.

Marvin, though, had the same experience at Bingo. That was an impromptu gig for him. They didn't expect him there that night. There was Mrs. Crow, who had encouraged him in third grade, when she first heard his music, and there was Jameson who had tried to learn trombone but quit, and there was Lindsay, the first woman to be wooed by his playing. When Marvin played that night at Bingo, he put on the best show he had all year, and when they clapped and screamed for him, he was the real Marvin again.

Next week, he was due to speak at the local junior high and play a little there. He only hoped he could inspire the next generation with his playing.

He made his way home from Bingo, passing by the park. There was an excellent street-performer there that night – a trombone-player. Crowds had gathered around him and were dancing and clapping along. Marvin wasn't impressed and just kept walking. Whatever those crowds heard, he couldn't hear it. And when he got home, he went to sleep with a smile on his face.

Courtesy of his band's booking agent, Drew Lawrence happened to be in Cleveland that night, too. And he happened to pass that same trombone player.

And Drew Lawrence was also unimpressed; that player had no showmanship, sounded very outdated, and he wasn't very handsome, either. He was wearing suspenders, for Christ's sake. Drew Lawrence hurried along – he was on his way to another hotel room to meet with a reporter. Later on, he too fell asleep with a smile on his face.

That trombone player in the park told stories with the notes, created colors with the melodies, bared soul. Most people in a hurry stopped. Everyone smiled; everyone moved. People who didn't like trombone music, people who didn't usually like a particular cover – they all stayed until the end. He seemed to be at one with the music. It seemed to emanate out of him as if it was being created spontaneously from the deepest part of him.

He had played his whole life – for his family, for his co-workers, for strangers, for himself.

Everyone in the crowd was still thinking about his music as they got home – how it affected them, how it tied in with their lives, what it made them picture. And then they each realized that none of them even knew his name – they only knew his work. And they all fell asleep with smiles on their faces.

Kim Sedlock has a B.A. in Creative Writing from Beloit College, where she studied under Pulitzer nominee Clint McCown. She was first prize winner of their Lois and Willard Mackey Prize for her short stories, a contest that was judged by National Book Award Winner Bob Shacochis. She was first published at age fourteen, writing modern dance reviews in a New York newspaper. Her short story collection, A Thirteen-Story View, is poised to be published in 2021. She lives in Maine with her husband, where she is the sole playwright, stage director, and occasional performer for Pass the Pine Cones Theater Company, and where she teaches writing workshops.

About Mad Zebra Press

Mad Zebra Press is new on the scene. Our goal is to publish high-quality literature from not-yet-famous writers, including both short stories and poetry. Although we are based in Buffalo, N.Y., we publish work from writers all over the U.S.

Look for our upcoming publications in 2021, including *Remains: A Collection of Poetry* by Heather Richmond and *A Thirteen-Story View* by Kim Sedlock, which is a collection of short stories.

!((!

Mad Zebra Press
madzebrapress.com

www.ingramcontent.com/pod-product-compliance
Lightning Source LLC
Chambersburg PA
CBHW070425140726
47909CB00021B/2931

9780578783253